ANIMAL Eagle DIARIES

STEVE PARKER

NEW
BURLINGTON
BOOKS

A NEW BURLINGTON BOOK
The Old Brewery
6 Blundell Street
London N7 9BH

First published in the United States in 2013 by
QEB Publishing, Inc.
3 Wrigley, Suite A
Irvine, CA 92618
www.qed-publishing.co.uk

A CIP record for this book is available from the Library of Congress.

ISBN 978 1 60992 581 9

Project Editor Carey Scott
Illustrator Peter David Scott/The Art Agency
Designer Dave Ball
QED Project Editor Tasha Percy
Managing Editor Victoria Garrard
Design Manager Anna Lubecka

Printed and bound in China

Photo Credits
Key: t = top, b = bottom, l = left, r = right, c = center,
FC = front cover, BC = back cover.
Alamy Tierfotoagentur/A. Brillen 11, David Gowans 28 **Shutterstock** 5,
John A. Anderson 12t, Maxim Petrichuk 15 br, Zacarias Pereira de Mata
18t, Maksimilian 20b; Gordan, David M. Scrader, Luminis, Oleg Golovnev,
Ana de Sousa, Valentin Agapov, Dementeva, Petr Jilek all background
images

Contents

You may admire my regal profile.

Best Nest

I saw the sun rise for the second time today. That means I must be two whole days old! My fluffy feathers have dried out after being in that damp egg for six weeks, but I'm still testing my tiny wings and legs. Stre-e-e-tch.

Mother's tail is spread, ready to land.

Brother pecks to get out.

Golden Eagle

Group Birds—raptors (birds of prey)

Adult length 3 feet

Wingspan 7.2 feet

Weight Female 13 pounds, male 9 pounds

Habitat Mountains, hills, moors, plains, open woods

Food Small to medium-sized mammals, birds, frogs, sometimes fish and snakes

Features Large eyes with powerful sight, hooked beak, strong talons

Here comes Mother. She says golden eagles are the most noble and important of all birds. We are "feathered royalty." So Mother's a queen, Father's a king—and I'm a princess!

Stork's nest is on a house chimney!

I'm still tired from hatching —it took me almost two days!

Eagles build nests, called eyries, in sensible places like crags, cliffs, or trees. Some other birds make their nests in very peculiar positions—like rafts floating in rivers.

I'm Hungry

Aweek has passed since my first diary entry, and I'm becoming fond of Brother. At first he pushed and pecked me. But I'm bigger now and I can peck and scratch harder than him.

The loudest squawker gets the most mouthfuls!

When a parent arrives we open our beaks wide, flap our tiny wings, and squawk loudly. It's called begging. When I grow bigger, I'll be such an important princess that lesser eagles will beg to me!

Today's meal is ~~doormat~~ ~~moormot~~ marmot. It's soft and juicy. I also like pigeon, goose, and lizard. Being a royal princess, I am used to the very best ~~kwizine~~ cuisine.

Yellow-bellied Marmot

Group Mammals—rodents

Adult length 18 inches, plus 6 inch tail

Weight Up to 11 pounds

Habitat Hills, mountain meadows, grassland, woodland edge

Food Grass, flowers, buds, seeds, roots, insects, worms, birds' eggs

Features Long, sharp front teeth for gnawing, thick fur, strong claws to dig burrows for hibernation

THIS WEEK'S MENU

Greater sage grouse is one of our biggest meals.

American pika is a tender snack.

Mountain cottontail can be a bony meal.

Muskrat makes a musky smell and tastes muddy.

Swoop to Kill

Brother and I had a great view yesterday of Mother catching a meal in mid-air. She spotted a mallard duck flying far below. I saw her dip her head, curve back her wings, and dive at incredible speed.

1. Mother preparing to dive.

Duck was flapping fast.

2. Wings back for extra speed.

Duck dives down, but not fast enough.

She swooped down from above and behind the duck, so it couldn't see her. Then, she stretched out her feet, spread her toes, and . . .

Wham! She thudded into the duck, speared it with her pointed toe claws, called talons, and brought it back to Noble Nest to share with us. It was a great lesson. I'm going to learn to be just as fierce. Marvelous Mother!

Feathers for my royal diary!

4. Wing feathers spread to carry heavy prey.

3. In go the deadly talons.

Alone Again

I'm a month old now, and very sad. Brother disappeared last night. I think he died and my parents took his body away. I admit that I did boss him around now and then, but we were nest-mates and I'll miss him loads.

I want feathery legs like Father's!

Father explained that Brother died because he was too small and weak. He says that often only one eaglet survives in a Goldie nest. So I'm the lucky one in this family.

My talons are growing big and sharp.

As my fluffy baby down feathers fall out, I practise preening my new, golden adult ones. How very regal I look!

The loss of Brother means more food for me!

Spread your feathers well so your beak and claws can get between them, down to the skin.

PREENING FOR BEGINNERS

Keeping your feathers clean, combed and tidy is called preening. It's one of the most important skills for any bird. It gets rid of dirt and also pests like fleas and ticks on feathers and skin. It also arranges your feathers neatly so they form a smooth area with no gaps, which you need for safe flight.

Remember: preen every day when you wake up, after meals and before bedtime.

Cougar

Group Mammals—carnivores

Adult length Female 6 feet, male 8 feet, plus tail

Weight Up to 220 pounds

Habitat Snowy mountains, rocky hills, woods, swamps, dry scrub, farmland

Food Animals from frogs, mice, and rats to fish, birds, porcupines, deer

Features Long, sharp front teeth, good eyesight and hearing, fast reactions, sharp claws, long, twitching tail

Near Miss

Today I had my first taste of real danger. Dozing in Noble Nest, I heard a rustle and a scrape. I'm supposed to stay low down in the nest, but curiosity got the better of me— I just had to take a peek!

My big squawk gave Crouchy a shock!

uh-oh! I should have taken my parents' advice and stayed low down.

Shriek, screech—Crouchy the Cougar! He'd scrambled up the rocks in search of lunch—me! I flapped and squawked, and, luckily for me, he just couldn't hang on.

EAGLE ENEMIES

Lynx is similar to Crouchy.

Wolverine is truly fierce—respect!

Coyote howls at night.

Gray wolf never gives up a chase.

Ears back meant Crouchy was ready to kill.

I hope his cubs don't try too!

Paw pads could not grip.

Crouchy tumbled down the rocks, bumping and bashing. If he tries to get back up here again, I'll be ready to give him a royal jab to the nose!

Claws slipped on damp rock.

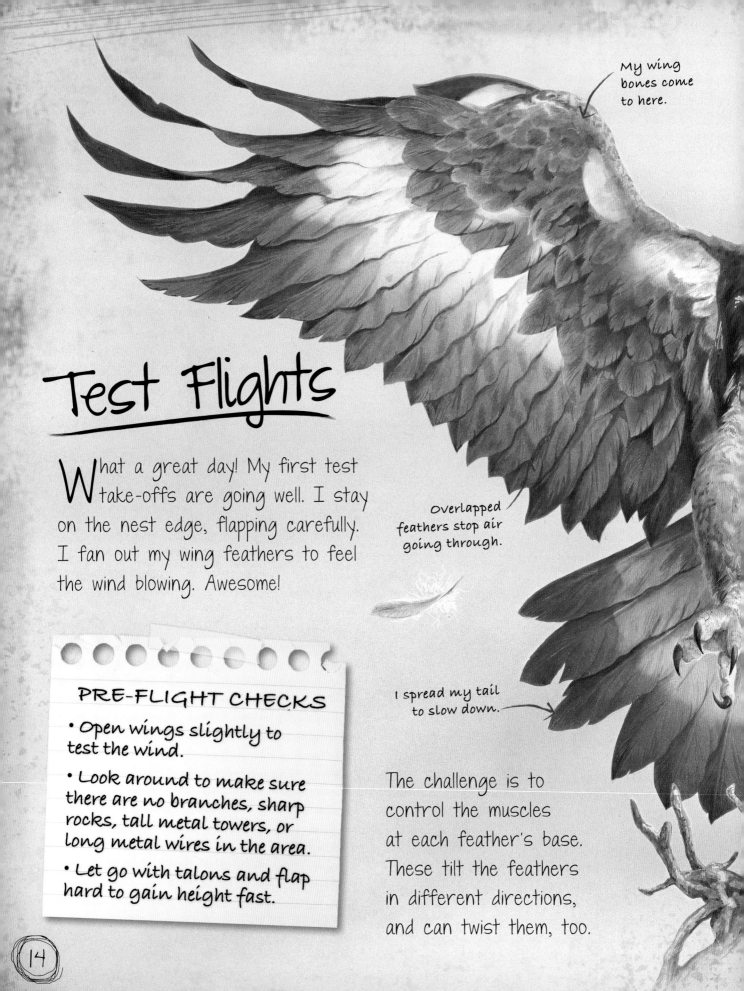

My wing bones come to here.

Test Flights

What a great day! My first test take-offs are going well. I stay on the nest edge, flapping carefully. I fan out my wing feathers to feel the wind blowing. Awesome!

Overlapped feathers stop air going through.

I spread my tail to slow down.

PRE-FLIGHT CHECKS

• Open wings slightly to test the wind.

• Look around to make sure there are no branches, sharp rocks, tall metal towers, or long metal wires in the area.

• Let go with talons and flap hard to gain height fast.

The challenge is to control the muscles at each feather's base. These tilt the feathers in different directions, and can twist them, too.

Whoosh, that was close. A gust of wind almost blew me away. But with the freedom of flight, I'll soon be soaring high above my empire!

Twisting my feathers makes me turn.

I stayed close to the nest edge.

KNOW YOUR FEATHERS

As an eagle, you have several kinds of feathers. On your body are contour feathers for warmth, protection, streamlining, and color. Under these are soft fluffy down for extra warmth. Your wings have two kinds of feathers, called primaries and secondaries.

Primary feathers help you move through the air.

Body feathers lie flat and even.

Secondary feathers give lifting force.

Up and Away

Flying so high, I can keep watch over a huge area for prey and danger. Looking down to the canyon, I spy a chance to catch my first splendid feast! I'll follow those ~~dear~~ deer to see if one of them is sick or injured.

My eyes take up more head space than my tiny bird brain!

I'm learning how to keep my head steady even though my body and wings tilt and twist in the wind. That means my eyes can stay fixed on the target—in this case a small deer with a bad leg.

My eagle eyes zoom in on this wounded youngster.

Eagles are not called eagle-eyed for nothing! Our eyes have a magnifying middle area, so that things look bigger and nearer. My eagle eyes can spot a mouse from a mile away, so this deer looks like a real giant.

The buck (male) is too big and strong for me.

White-tailed Deer

Group Mammals—hoofed mammals

Adult length Up to 7 feet

Weight Up to 330 pounds

Habitat Mostly woods and forests, also shrubland, rocky hills, dry scrub

Food Plants from grasses and cactus to mosses, mushrooms, and tree bark

Features Good sight and hearing, long legs, white underside, male has large antlers

First Big Kill

Yesterday's deer hunt did not end well. The ~~heard~~ herd went into a thick forest and I could no longer see them. So today I went soaring again. I was very careful because Wolf Pack were on the prowl.

Wolves sometimes steal my catch.

Snowshoe Hare

Group Mammals—rabbits, hares, and pikas

Adult length 20 inches

Weight 3.3 pounds

Habitat Open woods and forests, grasslands, farmland, swamps

Food Plants from mosses, buds and leaves to seeds, twigs, and bark

Features Long, sharp front teeth, powerful back legs, thick fur that turns from brown to white in winter

After almost a day in the air, I saw a Snowshoe Hare nibbling grass on a rocky slope. Awesome! I swooped down, then saw that Wolf Pack were also on Snowy's trail. No time to waste!

Like Mother, I curved my wings to dive and spread my talons. I stabbed Snowy and flapped hard to carry away my kill. The Pack were just behind, but they could not catch the princess of the skies!

TALON STRENGTH

Your beak and talons are both hunting weapons. Talons are also vital for perching, preening, and holding food while you tear bits off. Look after them!

	POWER OF GRIP	BENDINESS	SENSE OF TOUCH
EAGLE TALONS	9/10	2/10	5/10
HUMAN HANDS	4/10	8/10	9/10

My wings took the hare's weight.

Snowy's white feet were really easy to spot.

Eagle Encounter

This morning, I was quietly ripping up and gulping down a wild goat I'd caught. When I looked up—there was Whitehead. He's an eagle too, but he's not regal like me.

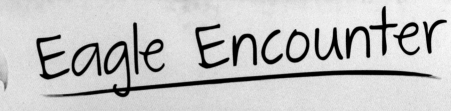

Bald Eagle

Group Birds—raptors (birds of prey)

Adult length 3.3 feet

Wingspan 7 feet

Weight Female 13 pounds, male 9 pounds

Habitat Rivers, lakes, swamps, coasts

Food Small to medium-sized animals, especially fish and waterbirds

Features White feathers on head and neck, hooked yellow beak

Rough toe skin for grabbing slippery fish.

Why Whitehead is called a Bald Eagle, I do not know. Maybe from a long distance, animals with poorer eyesight than mine could mistake his white feathers for bare skin.

BALD EAGLE VS. GOLDEN EAGLE

BALD EAGLE
- Prefers open water, like a lake, big river, or the coast.
- Loves to catch fish and shore creatures like gulls and crabs.
- Sometimes steals food from other birds—even from us Goldies!

GOLDEN EAGLE
- Likes drier areas with grass, rocks, bushes, and scattered trees.
- Eats mainly mammals and birds, rarely fish.
- Usually catches own prey, but also scavenges on dead bodies.

We chatted for a while and compared catches. Whitehead likes fish best. I catch a few fish, but the small bones are awkward to swallow. Whitehead also grabs turtles from the water.

I flap my wings so I can pull with extra ripping power.

My hooked beak tears off lumps of goat—yum!

The goat is heavy, so I'll eat it here.

Bear Facts

My first winter has been tough work. Many of the creatures I usually catch are hiding in their ~~borruws~~ burrows or sheltering in the forest. Yesterday I soared over Stony Mountain and noticed a strange shape in a snowy clearing. I plunged down fast and . . .

Wolvey has amazing, bone-crunching teeth.

I screeched, but no luck.

. . . saw it was a dead bighorn sheep. What a feast! I landed nearby and checked all was clear. Wolverine appeared from the bushes but I flapped and shrieked to keep her away. She can crunch up the leftovers.

I backed away from Grizzly.

Grizzly found the sheep by smell.

The sheep slipped and fell.

Disaster! Grizzly strolled into the clearing and made a ground-shaking growl. As ruling princess of the birds, I can frighten off most other animals, but not Grizzly. No sheep for me this time so it's back to searching from the sky.

Grizzly Bear

Group Mammals—carnivores

Adult length 6.5–8.5 feet

Weight Up to 1,100 pounds

Habitat Forests, woods, mountains

Food Animals from frogs and fish to big deer and sheep; many plants especially fruits, nuts, and berries

Features Enormous size, massive paws with long claws, excellent hearing and smell, white tipped hairs give old or "grizzled" appearance

Howdy, Partner

Strong wings with no feather gaps.

It's the first time I've written in my diary for three years! I left Muther and Father's territory when I was nearly two. Then it took me another two years to find my own territory, where I could live, hunt, and rest. But few birds like to live alone, and today I found a partner.

THE IDEAL PARTNER – WHAT TO LOOK FOR:

1. Well-preened plumage.
2. Smooth, powerful wing beats.
3. Good balance when walking and hopping.
4. Bright, clear eyes.
5. Strong talon grip.
6. Healthy appetite.
7. Loud screech to warn of danger.

Talons without chips or nicks.

Another Goldie flew past a few times, too high for me to worry about. Then it came past lower, and again, even lower. I saw it was a male. It's now spring and we both feel the need to mate. So we began our courtship.

Golden eagle partners usually stay together year after year until one dies. This is called "mating for life."

IMPRESSING A PARTNER

Courtship shows a possible partner that you are fit and well, and will make a good parent; one who's able to raise a healthy family. Of course, the partner must also impress you. Try these great courting moves:

• **Roller-coaster** Fly in an up-and-down way, climbing and then diving, as fast as you can.
• **Present-drop** Dive to the ground, pick up a stone, twig, or pebble, fly high in the sky, drop it, power-dive to catch it in mid-air. Repeat up to five times.
• **Talon-lock tumble** Grasp each other's talons then both somersault over and over as you plunge downward.

I'm liking the look of him!

I'm showing off my evenly spaced wing feathers.

He flew at me. I flew at him. We held talons, swooped up and down, shrieked and called, "Caw!" We played with presents for each other. It was lots of fun and we agreed to become the new queen and king of Stony Mountain.

25

Our New Territory

When Eddie and I became a pair, we needed a larger territory where we could both hunt. So we teamed up and chased away the eagles next door. Now we have enough land to live on.

cliff ledges make fine nest sites.

I started my tour over Thick Forest.

I keep an eye on Grizzly!

Today I flew over our territory to find some good nest ~~sights~~ sites. We need somewhere quite high, but not so far up a mountain that it's always cold and windy. Sheltered cliff ledges and tall trees are best.

My wings are too long to fly among trees. I'll stay above them.

The nest site should be difficult for predators to reach, especially bears, big cats, and wolverines. I still shudder when I remember how Crouchy climbed up to Noble Nest when I was just an eaglet!

I'll stay clear of these tall trees with strange, spinning branches.

Ravens mobbed me!

The wind blowing up the slope lifted me higher.

This tree is a possible nest site.

Crystal Lake

After my territory tour, I met Eddie on Stony Mountain. We talked about the best nest sites and decided on four. We use only one each year, but we make spares in case the first nest gets destroyed.

Eddie waited for me.

Eaglets of Our Own

Today is so royally important! Our first eaglets hatched and we both feel so proud of our new princess and prince! But now it gets busy. Eddie and I will be out all hours finding food for them both.

Eddie arrives with our next meal—a hare.

GOLDEN EAGLETS HATCH OUT

Eaglet One waits for Eaglet Two to emerge

Mountains Weekly announces that the Golden Eagle pair of Big Tree, near Crystal Lake, have two new babies. Both eaglets and their parents are doing well. But this means the Mother and Father will be busy over the coming weeks, hunting for extra food. So we warn all rabbits, hares, mice, voles, marmots, and birds, from sparrows to swans, to take extra care. Sign up to our Online Eagle Alert to see when they swoop over your area. And remember the Golden Eagle Rule—Keep One Eye on the Sky!

I remember when I was young and shared the nest with Brother. Only I survived. Now we also have two eaglets, Eddie and I will try our best to take good care of them, so they both grow up and leave the nest.

EAGLET CHECK LIST

1. Feed eaglets only small pieces, or they may choke.

2. Remove their droppings every day.

3. Warn them to keep low and stay quiet!

I tore up a marmot as food.

This year's great weather means plants are growing well. So our prey have plenty to eat, which means lots of food for us. The Royal Family's future looks good!

Eaglet One is big and begs best.

Eaglet Two is also strong and healthy.

What They Say About Me

My diary describes what I think about all the creatures I meet. But what do they think about me? Let's find out . . .

Grizzly Bear

> Goldies hiss and squawk, but they don't scare me, and nor does Cougar. In fact, nothing scares me because I'm the true King of the Mountains!

White-tailed Deer

> Sure, eagles catch a few of us who are old or ill. But honestly, it's OK. Those deer would only slow down the main herd. No, it's fine, really . . .

> Nasty Eagle who swoops down from nowhere is our worst enemy. So is Cougar who pounces silently. And Wolverine, and Grizzly, and . . .

Marmot

Bald Eagle

> I would have more time and respect for the Golden Eagles if they dropped all that rubbish about being the Royal Family. Everyone knows that I am the great bird symbol of power and strength.

> I almost caught that royal Goldie when she was an eaglet, but she slipped through my paws. I hear she's got eaglets of her own now. Tempting!

Cougar

Tricky Terms

Bighorn A type of North American wild sheep with long, curly horns.

Buck A male deer, antelope, or similar hoofed animal.

Burrow A long hole like a tunnel dug by a creature, where it can hide, rest and sleep.

Contour feathers Flat feathers on a bird's body that make its shape smooth and streamlined, to pass through the air easily.

Courtship A display by an animal to show willingness to mate with its partner.

Eyrie An eagle's nest, usually built in a tree or on a high ledge.

Mobbing When a group of similar animals, such as birds, gather to make loud noises and pretend to attack a larger predator, to scare it away.

Nest site A place where a bird or similar animal makes its "home" or nest, to rest and sleep in, and perhaps to raise young.

Plumage All the feathers of a bird including their sizes, shapes, colors, and patterns.

Prey A creature that is caught and eaten by another, the hunter, or predator.

Primaries Large, long feathers at the ends, or tips, of a bird's wings, which can fan out and tilt to control flight.

Raptors General name for the birds of prey group, which have sharp, hooked beaks and long sharp claws, and hunt other creatures to eat. The main day-flying kinds are eagles, hawks, buzzards, falcons, vultures, and condors, and at night, owls.

Secondaries Medium-sized feathers in rows along a bird's wings, that provide the main area for lift (upward force) and thrust (forward force) when flying.

Streamlining A smooth, curved shape, without sharp corners or protruding parts, which slips easily though air or water.

"Tall trees with spinning branches" Eagle's name for wind turbines, which humans build to turn the blowing force of the wind into electricity.

Talons Strong, sharp, curved claws, such as on the toes of a bird of prey.

Territory An area where an animal lives, feeds, and breeds, and which it defends against others of its kind.

Wolf pack A group of wolves that live and hunt together, with one female and male in charge.

> Hares and rabbits everywhere must always look out for eagles. We call them the Winged Killers because they have wings and they kill us. Obvious, really.

Snowshoe Hare

Index